SPOOKS

S T E L L A W O N G

saturnalia | BOOKS

Distributed by Independent Publishers Group
Chicago

Saturnalia Books
105 Woodside Rd.
Ardmore, PA 19003
info@saturnaliabooks.com

ISBN: 978-1-947817-38-8 (print), 978-1-947817-39-5 (ebook)
Library of Congress Control Number: 2021947064

Cover art by Ilya Milstein
Book design by Robin Vuchnich

Distributed by:
Independent Publishing Group
814 N. Franklin St.
Chicago, IL 60610
800-888-4741

For My Mother

TABLE OF CONTENTS

PINEAPPLE

Lucy Liu, don't worry,
I remember you
from the movie
Chicago where
Richard Gere said
your mother owned all
the pineapples
of Hawaii because
of course
with the surname Baxter,
you'd be an American
Kitty, bastardized roots
for this yellow fruit.
You'd be the most far-out
almost foreign
villain/villanelle sweet-
heart of America. I wonder
if, in addition to kneeing
two guys, you felt something break
your mother's heart, captured
in your sights
the faces of the man and women of
America cheating on
the imperiled overrich.
You teach me how to act

imperial. Overreach.
Act as if gold-
medalled, first-
prized for what
lines you land,
which marks you flay.
Lucy Liu, you are no
dragging lady
of the spouse.
Sidekick,
take the addict
and make a detective
out of Sherlock.
Joan Watson,
you are kōan
and kingmaker
and go on
not as an
othered best friend
but as a game changer.
Also Lucy Liu,
you are good
at being the head
of a crime ring.
Lucy Liu, you've had

no real need
to keep
a ring of men around
you. O-Ren,
they're dead
meat as you see
the white woman
in a yellow skin-
tight suit
can really pick them
off, easy. You're the hit
list's top billing.
When she beheads you,
plant your crown.
Your trunk will grow back
where you went down.
You show me
I can come
to fruition
and yellow on my own
terms.
Lucy Liu do not stay
silent this is not
an old black-and-
white. You are well

within your rights.
You can feel free
to be bad
and reel
me in.
If you can act
then I can act out.
This is not your death
scene. You can afford
to take the heads off
everyone in the room
and not leave them in
one piece. If they will
remember you for your murder
why not make a killing.

WHO'D ROB GOD?

You break it you pay for it.

I'm so very bored with all my jesuses today.
I already talked to them in a baby voice
and by them, I mean all of them
baby jesuses I stole from target.

I targeted each and every one—
I lifted them. I lifted them from the shelf.
Shoplifted? I'd rather not,
that word's no fun

at all. They were just, wow,
so funny looking. You know how medieval babies
were really just full size men
or how cherubs are ambiguously sexed?

Maybe I'll talk to my jesuses in my daddy voice next.

FU ER DAI

Last year, the son of China's richest man posted pictures online of his
dog wearing two gold-plated Apple Watches, one on each front paw.
—*"China's Rich Kids Head West," The New Yorker*

This winter I just had
to wing it—dinner
with two boys
from Guangzhou,
from two generations
where legacies run
un-hijacked. In electric orange sweatshirts
the color of a parent's guilt,
each hole silk-patched on
GIVENCHY-stenciled
chests, they fought
about the worth
of the proletariat
and the meaning of nice
clothes. I wore my
mother's worn shoes
five sizes up
and my mother's
face, a show all made-up
for my mother's guests,
an established institution

on New Years' Eve.
On gold-lettered tablets,
they scrolled down
characters I didn't know.
Ancient Chinese poetry,
they explained, was perfect
symmetry—bloodlines of
words and verbs twinned
like an airshow of bombers
and blue angels.
I wondered how they found
my limping
tongue and second-hand
guessing, a child of
a one-child policy
in an unamended family,
moth-eaten custody
split between two bodies.
Instead, I covered with
my mouth the hole
in my sleeve.

BANDAIDS DIDN'T MAKE A COLOR FOR ME, OR THINKING INSIDE THE BOX, OR CRAYON WITHIN THE LINES

Where do you put your body
of color

Where do you put
your body of color

Where do you put
your color of body

Where do you put
your off-color body

Where do you color
your body on

Where do you put off
your body

Where do you put
on your body

What do you color
of your body

Where do you body
your color

Where you off-put
you, there you are:

You are body.
You are color.

POMELO

In my kitchen, some white man
        shouts, what is this? R tells him it's a pomelo,

interrogates the fruit like the cops
        with Buddha

in custody—head
        old and wrinkled.

For my grandmother, held up
        (after the flight

home, after the funeral)
        in customs, has survived

much more than is custom to speak. Imported bride
        of little import.

When I head out for the pomelo,
        the fallen alien has landed

defaced, branded
        by fingernails, some cruel

curiosity of the bright.
        Yellow hide carrying white man-

made mottles that look (in spite
        of the gossip that is not gospel)
        like dimples.

I carry my baby to the bar
        because I can't drink. Buddhist, I say,

or pregnant. A colonizer insists we split it,

carving the fruit into spheres of influence.
        What color is it? asks his girlfriend.

We're all pink on the inside. She almost chokes
        on her laughter

and no one realizes that
        I am not talking about the meat.

NOT YOUR BERNINI'S DAPHNE

after Christo + J-C's "Wrapped Trees", Basel, Germany

I wish I were a real tool,
not Pinocchio nor

Father of god
tinkerer

who lies about
lying with

structures
at his disposal.

What kind of father
has a child

and lets him run around
a tree?

If the child had a mother
figure, she'd have

him human
in no time at all.

Let me be
instrumental. In this

reanimation,
my mother is Penelope

looming nightmares
of an unwound shroud

to mummify
the family tree.

I wish I were turbine,
o telekinetic superheroine.

To please
Mother, sap the ichor.

Rub Lethe's genie
bottled with two x's.

Tango and spar
all stars. Don't weave

in crowns
for a hollow king.

Fuck that noise.
I destroy the nest.

Come bless your woodwind
with a mouth to speak.

I will sing out your victory.

PYRAMID SCHEME

Are we sick for trying
to get me gainful

employment from old men
and laughing?

Pouring olive oil
over white rice with a single raw tomato,

pink salt and pepper, we dream
of infinite ways to make my vagina and hair

a bulletproof slot machine, mostly plotting
for people to fall in love with my feet

or selling merengue color eyeshadow
which is 10% metal, 90% aspiration

(my beauty secret is starting fights
at parties I'm the host of).

Cleopatra was always becoming—and that
was the source of her kingdom.

If ours is built from lying
in the ruins, puppeteering the pharaohs,

I disguise my panic in your reassurance:
Of course, my horse. In an emergency, eat the rich.

We're getting good at make believe, that
making love is coming soon to a theatre near you.

Don't pause this movie yet. It's getting good
at saying sorry for your loss. Poring over

family albums of Martha's Vineyard
dock swims and wine legs, over

the meal we improvise from a Markov generator
about how to eat if I'm depressed,

faith works its boiling magic.
It's messy jokes—how to carry this godly computer worm

(over-the-shoulder like a fireman's hose)
and distraction from our foolish hunger

when love is watching
the compounds break down.

EVERYTHING ABOUT YOU IS OFFENSIVE EXCEPT YOUR CAT

after "The Thousand-Hand Bodhisattva"

A pop singer populates
her songs with geishas, poplar-tall, all

stilts and prayer
hands and sexual.

Katy Perry, in time
I learned all things white

have their own rules: crazy turns
to eccentricity. Zealous to the elect.

Fetish to something
like respect.

Like her popularity, her yellowface
and hello kitty obsession will be

forgotten by the lucky cat's wave.
What is not lost: us double-exposed

shots with a blur
of wholly curious palms

and a curated summer playlist held together
by popsicle sticks and a prayer

to a goddess
who looks

nothing like their savior. What is more
sacred than

a thousand arms
born gold

like me,
dancing on

one hand,
playing

myself with
all the rest.

BYE BYE

*after "American Pie," sung by Leslie Cheung, a Cantopop star who died
jumping off the 24ᵗʰ floor of the Mandarin Oriental hotel, Hong Kong*

boys always
        haunting the gas

stationed at
        the kum and go

come around yelling
        happy july, all

these lives you haven't filled
        in all these teeth

a faith so deep you can
        die in it, like a boy so

high up he thought the
        swimming pool was full

and god willing, he
        dived in it. in a

preemptive strike, patriotic, *partirons*
        and party on! miss 中国

in 中西部,
     i dismiss

their existence, a flotilla
     with more in common

with a root beer vanilla
     concoction than the

spanish armada, though
     that too was a whipped

cream loss. dq stands
     for disqualification—three

strikes and the cup is half
     mosh pit half military

campaign – *god is in the*
     good fizz – and the bottom

(beyond the caffeine and
     fresh sugarcane) is concrete.

There's an eagle that has
usually
one child.

If it has two it will choose
only
one to take

care of, and purposefully
mistreat the other
so it dies.

The bigger sibling pecks
the little one so he's more shitty
looking.

So the parents feed the bigger
one and they eventually ditch
the little one in the middle

of nowhere. So it dies.
And so it goes.
I would peck you now if I could.

Peck you on the cheek.

On the cheek until

        the cheekbone was exposed.

     I feel like you would look good
eating red Jello.

       You know

     red Jello is made from gelatin,
bone?

       I'll enjoy

     my ride in
to hell now.

       Next to all the writers from the Inquisition.

ANTIMATTER

I'm taken as an only child
  with multiverses. There's nothing

worse than the sense of being alone. Out there.
  In here. There's a reason

only's only two letters away from lonely.
  An l and an e. Le, an article starting at the

beginning. One particle searching for its
  other. Or Ēl, inhumanly. An eve without

man. A night without a man. Who? Any
  human. Do I carry within me both man and

woman, dialectic newborns? Or is there
  another male other out there who

stands by in silence as I swear? Does it
  matter? What does? There is

matter and antimatter carrying within
  itself the ability to destroy the other as

they meet.

SEARCH ENGINE

i.

move to this belly-up country
with only a roll of hawthorn tokens

in my pocket. mouth
always out of it.

my old friends, now
poofed away, redefine

a well-known rural game.
tractorfuckers.

ii.

walk white students through
the incantation

of my name, race white
faculty through the same,

erased because white boards
always stay that way.

recant, relabel,
decant cabs for the job. remain

unheard by the ears
of corn. scan the tight-lipped leaves.

always cropped
of familial characters. read myself

silly, missing subject
in a sentence, sentenced

to my sweet illusion. my magician
the cashier winks in collusion

at my candied 山楂 flakes. the last few
images must be staged.

iii.

this is the game:
pipe down and

exhaust the spell
that hypnotizes the fields.

in the lonely aisles, pry
last year's yield from ghostly sleeves:

prizes seen through a sleight of hand,
prepare fuchsia fruits to

cape for yet another
prop sawed through

too many times.
scape and scrap this goat,

chew out, chew through the handcuffs
to open sesame. polish off

all the names you'll have
recognized—branded White Rabbits,

大白兔奶糖 mute and boundless
in their dissolving rice paper,

solving a metal mother
land's milk, soy

as weak as i am, made palatable
for the intolerant.

iv.

get informed
scarecrow,

escapist, for a form
of abracadabra now:

you wouldn't like me
here without culture

except for kombucha and yogurt,
the lessen i bring to the community

potluck. buy a pot, have no more
luck for myself.

tokenism, that's a wrap
of catharsis in a magic trick.

MODES OF PRODUCTION

Donor, do no harm. Remain
harmonious, do you promise,
on your honor? You're single. Your single,
your song, your organ's tune
organic from your body's you
the you we want to breach and
breed, if you'll have us, it's easy
just check this box. We'll have
egged you on, but well it'll take
even if the baby's breech, our word's
our Word: and as for you, make you swear
hand on bible, box in air.

HOW CAN YOU TELL IF IT'S RIPE YET?

We haven't yet opened the corn hiding
on my side of the car console that you stole

from Monsanto. What a name, as if mon
santé for health or a dinnertime cheers, or

mi santo, my saint of another name,
could only be bastardized. No, the extra

o! turns the communion dastardly as if the
custard turned out to be thickened with

christ's blood after all, or the hero is
revealed to be the villain – we've all seen

that movie. According to the pictures (and
the music video), corn waves gold like an oasis or

an evil genie or temptress, but all that speeds by is
green. The stench is bad too—something

rotten this way comes, Halloway would have
seen it from miles away, like a Gotham

built on a swamp, but no wait that's Virginia,
maybe D.C. Not the comics, the seat

of government. I'm told the smell is the pesticide
we've come to enjoy the taste of. But I digress. The perplexing

complex tattooed on the librarian's arm turns
out to be the blueprints for the Chartres labyrinth,

and instead of a Halloween themed corn maze
I float the idea by the hive mind of renaming

them to maize maze. But never mind, it's a bit
too ethnic for the Midwest. How about *you*
navigate that next time.

GO BIG OR GO HOME

Have you noticed recently
that due to an influx

of money and science
or money and the human need to rhyme

themselves a disproportionate number
of film stars are having twins?

Maybe it's more financially
efficient, like a two for one

deal or when you
cry extra hard at therapy

to get it all out in one go.
Therapy, one of the few

places I can't escape the music
that other people push

the buttons to
my future. Husband,

maybe I don't want to
bury my body, I'd rather have

a headache, Zeus styled
and brain a birth.

The therapist said I'd
need a disorder to keep talking

and insurance wouldn't
count marital problems as one.

I thought despair came
in twos, paired

off like a missing period, pregnant
with loss.

See, despair is really born
from *sperare*, hope

blistered as Athena's spear.
Inject my pain here.

To birth two brains, two for oh,
it's not one heart for me

and one for you, it's more—
oh, love is at no

cost to you, and it falls
on me to be the hero.

TO BEAR FALSE WHITENESS

after bunte götter — die farbigkeit antiker skulptur

as a programmer, it's that time of year
again to re-decolonialize google
and other western diseases.

the search engineers history
itself, and this one's a chronic
labyrinth where the hero is the antihero

and the cloistered beast is white too.
of course, the heroine sells out
the patriarch for the patriarchy. classic

supply and demand, more, amore, a moray
eel. speaking of race
to the bell, the lecturer's jaw unhinges

and no one bothers to school her; the greeks
rendered gods
with compounds built from ground jewels and burnt bone,

who were stripped by plebian archeologists
of their war paint. whitewash the profane
and call it sacred.

curricula is a standard cutup
stick em up highlight
reel and then some

didn't realize some
had Othered time-
lines drawn in other countries' sands

bound in linen and lemon, not just
pterodactyls, wooly mammoths and the few monstrous
world wars (and fallout).

it's been a minute
but she needs to lay off the chemicals
for her newest homeopathic therapy;

none dyed, no making up—
clothes leeched of assured color, Ice Age hair,
snowy eyelashes. the first positive ghost.

some more white bull.

WHEN THE STILL BREATHING WATCH THE STILL-BORN

after life

He was born in the year of the dog,
in the Zodiac
that means faithful,

and he is indeed full of faith.
Dogmatic, persistent
that we have

since the beginning ridden
the same wavelength
and can go on.

One-note campaigner
and godly
lyre-player.

When I was little it was my dream to ride
a big dog like a little horse.
That was before

I was dragged around a room by my feet
with my face to the floor,
like Hector around Troy,

like laps
around a pool
and well, I never wanted to experience

that particular circle of hell
again.
He'll find the waves

by the Golden Gate
Bridge to be holy. Speaking
of which, gottem!

What a misnomer. No gates, no gold,
just a bridge people find
it romantic to jump off of

to their deaths. No net
because the city finds it
unaesthetic.

But this isn't about me.
It's not either at face
value even about you

and the waves that abuse these black rocks
that are unendingly moving, re-
ceding to the

ether from which they came. You think no one hears
the SEALs
during Hell

Week in an exercise in excising
weakness when they line up
down in the liminal

space between sand and wave,
purgatory, flagellated—
arms linked to make a drawbridge

to drown or fend off
the naked lash's flog.
Orpheus, I too know the song.

BUDDHA DISCOVERS REINCARNATION AND REACHES NIRVANA UNDER THE FIG TREE'S HEART-SHAPED LEAVES

After 1910, the Angel Island Immigration Station was used to detain
Chinese immigrants due to the 1882 Chinese Exclusion Act. Many wrote
poetry on its walls and floors. The women's quarters burned down in 1940.

The fig wasp crawls.

The fig wasp crawls into
the fig plant's walls.

The fig wasp crawls inspins a little inversion
into the fig plant's walls.

The fig wasp won!
She's the first one in.

In Buddhism, nirvana *is translated as "extinguishing the flames of ignorance."*

The fig wasp wonders what
time is, where wonder went.

The fig wasp wonders where
time went, when wonder meant
one fermata moment—

but now the ferment has closed.

But now the ferment has closed down and
is all around her body.

But now the ferment has closed down
and is all around her *bodhi*.

Is she dying?

> The fig wasp's death is necessary for the production of the fruit;
> the wasp cannot lay eggs and dies alone.

This is *dhyana:* the fig meant no harm.

The fig meant *ahimsa* but inversion.

The fig meant *ahimsa*, but in this version,
inversion wouldn't be undone.

> In Sylvia Plath's The Bell Jar, *the narrator says, "I saw my life*
> *branching out before me like the green fig tree…the tip of every branch,*
> *like a fat purple fig, a wonderful…husband…and children…*

The fig wasp wandered
deep down in a nimbus.

The fig wasp wondered
if, deep within, she hadbecome a fig on her own.

> ...*I saw myself sitting in the crotch of this fig tree, starving to death.*"

The fig wasp in *nirvana*—
a figment of her own.

MULTIPLE WORLDS INTERPRETATION

What's the status of us?
You called it

a quantum state
when I wanted a word

not for the individual world
but the unit that it made.

Imagine in this earth's atmosphere,
a bag filled with air travels slowly in
the wind. On a jet stream, unearthly, air
can travel at hundreds of miles per hour.

Air can carry air very well.
Air can carry a bag filled with air,
a paper bag filled with not only air
that doesn't tear, a paper bomb filled with tears

and mass panic. Just as well
as a skin bag filled with air and manic
sound and fury. If the bag slips below
the jet stream, into the earth's sphere

a pin releases and
a smaller bag of sand is tossed off.
The bag rises, rises back into a place where
air carries air. The paper bags are made

with fear and care, paper fibers starched
with fury and parched by hand and patched –
with the handwritten pieces of letters – the holes where
the jet stream could announce itself,

like a stranger in a home,
like a bomb on a house.
Imagine several thousands paper bombs swimming
like minnows through air, high above a sea that separates

us from Japan, lands flung awry on
an open earth, where paper airplanes unload
pearls and paper bombs are sent to hurl
the fury that should have made it to

the papers, panic for
a protected people. Instead, because
America is a land of fields,
most of these hand-repaired paper

bombs land in fields or streams
and one in a forest where
a teacher on a field trip lets her caution go
to the wind, and picks paper with care

for the students to share.
And the sound unfurls
through the open earth, tearing a hole in
the normal order. The papers never report

the news, because air can carry panic
very well. Air can carry papers
very well. Air can carry air
very well. Imagine now, six souls, unbanded,

rise, rise up and travel in the wind.

OUTSIDE PARTY LINES

Cordelia, the deluge has nothing to do with you.
The doorman wants nothing to hear from you:
deliver the ice luge to the door out back.

Poor Delia of the doorbell ringing,
bells in a deluge gone blue from ringing,
bluebells are dying of water-lack.

Dear Delia, don't bring that news to bluegrass country.
Not in blue-sky, bud-light country.
Folk like that aren't welcomed back.

That's Delia who sees the ice luge change.
The neighbors left a carcass hanged
on her doorbell: just step back.

Yes Delia, you know the deluge is coming,
bluebirds gone singing and not coming
back. Bluebirds dying from water-lack.

Oh Delia, no one hears the lack of singing.
No one hears your doorbell-ringing,
the deluge wants nothing to do with you.

My Cordelia, named for the sea's daughter,
ever linked to Lear and slaughter.
You've seen the blue skies turn black.

WHILE I'M NOT A HEROIC COUPLET

America, I am not a negative
nor a positive. I am your zero

sum game, what I take you take
as stolen from you. My life is to be had

for a song, free as
America. To you I am nothing

but a number, O gasp, you are startled
I am still here. Oh a zero,

made by my Song ancestors
instead of leaving a space

on the page. J says,
it's American, not American't!

I disagree, it's the can as in trash,
I feel obliged to take myself out.

In time. America, I only wish
you would leave me

a space, at the very least
on paper, to sign.

I am still right
here.

QUID PRO NIL

The Red House restaurant is a farm-
to table type deal, and while I feel for caged chickens, I really do,
amidst the talk of alma mater basketball teams—

how well the young run on nothing
but thirst, prayer and well-oiled joints—
I'm not feeling it, this low bar
too unpresuming to be anything but a hole

in the wall. Over here, just seating two
in a long line of white-haired patrons
and the patronized, I can't help

but admire the historic patina of the
irony, it's got to be four or even five-stars,
that much like a small furred animal, gone
limp with fear and self-preservation

in the maw of a wildcat, my fingers are being held
down by yours. Rabbits
can cause their own hearts to explode and

I have never before wished so hard to be all ears,
but for the wandering forklift that seems to have picked up
on the proximity of my thigh. I feel for ciliced monks,
I really do. Skipping around the subject of men

who make me want to die, we proceed
to global health and health policy:
how to prevent suicide by gun

by making guns illegal. Or preventing oven deaths in Britain
by making oven gas nonlethal
which would have given Hansel and Gretel a hell
of an ending, I'm sure. Or preventing farmers from drinking

pesticides by making pesticides
nontoxic, in India, of all places—
I'm not here (that's how dissociative this fugue)

to incubate your cocksure ego. I mean really, my professor
transmogrified in a public place, and all
I got from it was three fun facts
about how to kill yourself.

HALLOWEEN

We do not buy
into crystals, poker

chips or other forms of bread
and circuses. We made ourselves up

in the mirror laced with rosary
and Mardi Gras beads, stranded

without the definition of fairy
lights, refusing to name ourselves
nympho, klepto, pyro.

We cannot afford the goose, cold
and blue and snow-white,

preferring to take it straight
from the mouth

of the next-door come-as-eurotrash party,
smoking the birthday boy out
of his self-imported cigarettes.

This is what I believe in:
my roommate's prayer-soft blanket

pleated in turquoise and other
shades of *please.* I believe we hail

voodoo utilized on ritualistic break-up,
one of us peeing on a pillow while
the other one pretends we cannot hear.

Let us say we are descended
from witches, have everything yet

to be maimed, too hot and too irregular to
live. I'll be your misshapen and your

mishaps will be mine, so scarce
and precious to be beloved. I see you,

hallowed queen folding sheets
some color other than white.

TO SCARE MEN

wear your neck
without necklaces

wear your ears
without earrings

wear your wedding
without wedding rings

women, no makeup.
without paint on

without mending
with four lives on

with four parents
without hair styled

with no sorries
with no toggling

with no begging
without amending—

NANJING 1937-38

after Iris Chang

I keep reliving
her own
World War
Two traumas
in which the name of a
popular band references
the prostitution sector
of a Nazi camp,
and the singer
commits suicide before
their first American tour.
Joy Division, indeed.
In which the writer of a book
with a child of her own
writes about the way the Japanese
made hookers of children
and conducted live experiments
on the childless that they
made child-less,
and she is harassed
night after night after night
for months and years

until people with something
to hide have remade her ears
and her eyes into another site of atrocity
and she takes her own life
and while the funeral
is held in Cupertino,
across the world a memorial
for victims of the massacre
makes for her a statue
and a cupid's wing.
Her child is two.

ADVOCACY

The avocados are lining the square. Do
you think they'll get shot, Garcia Marquez

style? Most choose not to think about it
because they don't need that kind

of negativity in their lives. Avocados with
a firm little black hood, avocados picked

up from their avocado lobbies and avocado
firms, avocados still-green, not knowing

where their avocado friends will end up. May-
be an avocado farm chasing rabbits? Most

likely an avocado camp in Siberia. Just-
ice is not green, but blind; rifles, sightless.

HALLOWEEN REDUX

In my photo there you are
girl, where you going

wearing that Trojan
centurion helmet

and wielding a trash can
heavy-lidded?

We vow to never have sex
and our empire never goes down

on us like the past. Quick

as a shot, you
stuff the embossed

helmet under your shirt,
as if smuggling his baby

robot dolls, medical diplomas and heavy
Mont-blanc pens

is the closest to hugging
and likewise shiny gifts

as only you can get.
As if stealing our IDs

gives you some face
value when we come to

you, lost. You tell us how
your doctor trash-talks, frames you

as asexual and crazy and even worse, poor
and we spin a webMD

diagnosis into fine compliment—
with bi-polar you've taken over

the whole world. How magnetic
you are, when you show off

your knees for the first time
forgiven by scars.

Let's toast to
us, the Last Triumvirate.

Your therapist has
eyes the exact shade of

vodka, never gives you a second shot
like we know how to do.

We know how to dance
to your maniac tune, stirring up

dust from the costume's
plumes. When we sneeze, you say you would

bless us but we've already been
with your presence, all disco, smoke and

three colognes. We are up
to our own devices, trumpeting

like Prometheus, what hell-colored
colonizer's hat we stole.

Let's be our own kings,
prom or drag.

If we're your other halves,
that makes you more than

holy—you,
in your photo, taken

after you admitted
us breaking

in the door—
you're half

somewhere
we don't know

beyond the frame. It is you
we are always in the process of winning

back, braced not by dagger nor bone
but the blood-red feathers

we carried back.

MATRYOSHKA

I had a dream
> where you brought me every single shoe I had ever dreamed
>> of. Metallic and jewel-toned. You
>>> said it was all for me.

I had a dream
> where the only thing I could think of was
>> why would you spend all of your income on
>>> shoes, metallic and jewel-toned? I started
>>>> to regret your maternal love.

I had a dream
> where I woke up, but it didn't matter
>> because the past was all metallic and jewel-toned, and
>>> you had brought me every single shoe I had
>>>> ever dreamed of.
>>>>> And I had been your doll.

And when I woke up,
> I was wearing your coat,
>> and that's two grand.

DEPORTATION

My roommate J has an alien feeling
so we compose
a rhapsody
in the key of
the wind's song. Without the haves
and the holds, and the holding
rooms, J prays
for some divine order.
Would they deport a butterfly, who knows
how to carry wishes
to the ears of gods.
We can pre-empt hope
itself, even better than genies.
Gold pilots alight on all three branches
of the oyamel fir tree.
Through the pane
of over-state-
meant, building on
trapped distraught monarchs.
What beautiful wallpaper
for the border wall.
A path to freedom
wraps around the paper's
weave. Apatheia comes

from below and above.
Negligence of the peat and the plant:
the pattern repeats
when caretakers are sent
to protect, but renege.
Royals leap
and are put to sleep *en masse.*
Is mass migration
an exigence or assassination?
What nation has walls
when the light is swallowed by night?
We have no need for your leave
to leave. Caped
crusaders
winging, winning out,
we're flying over
the wall—
lepidoptera
all asprawl.

THE SIGN FOR POWER

li 力
in Chinese

turned up-
side down

jackknifes into
the romanized

number four
or death.

I used
to be

a romantic,
used to use

a marker
to write on my wrist

the way
J

thinks we
cannot see

the smears
his magic

markers leave
behind

when he tries
shortcuts to

cut lines
on his legs.

He knights himself
without blade. 刀

draws on
a Cupid's bow

some braver source
to mark his growth

in lieu of new scars.
When what is ruined turns

white, the runes will be
visited. Our resident Aztec

doctor,
priest and

calendar-maker
derives his own

number 四 for
a suicide

hotline—
orange, hot

lines to call forth
power.

SPOOKS

(we begin bombing in 5 minutes)

I'm a rented lie
detector for the erotic subtext
in your shotgun nuptials. I know better

than to catch the MI5 in marsupial mode
proposing, won't you be the tote bag
to my red-handed dead drop?

I singlehandedly stop human agency
bloat by uninviting the stool pigeons
and other sand dollar informants.

The vows are three-legged nonsense
but they hold up better than a beached aviator
before the biblical flood. The jetset NSA confesses

to another blues singer tortured by the FBI— now I get totalitarian
cardboard props, vaccines, and Shark Week just so
someone's always Russian to your defense.

(disinformation tactics)

I can always count on State's dad
to quote Hamlet's dad after the breakup.
I'm a king cobra for love,

and I'm loving the sorrows that come
not in single spies but in battalions.
No one needs to hear it until after the Soviet Union

is outlawed. I'll keep all your blue Danube secrets
slow and remote until my battery runs out of acid.
It was I who set up the Berlin Wall

between my laws and in-laws – it's not good
for them to get ideas. In geopolitical terms,
I don't know what it means to be

on the fence: the OSS is checking out both of our exes
or exits. You never know where in China-Burma-India that guy is
puppetting his Pacific theater.

(anything else would be off-brand)

If you must read this out loud,
you can never take drug tests, hush money, or go

to church. I'm just an electric red honeymoon
away from honeypot boss. From the top,

Naval Intelligence likes writing oaths
to the wedding band's frontman

while tactically bombing
her latest marriage hard enough

to get through a military withdrawal.
Boy does the FSB dream of throwing a Molotov

cocktail hour, like Jesus. It's not my fault I'm hooked
on cabinets. But enough ministering. We go way back

to the CIA when there's not enough god in the water
to stop the gubernatorial headbangers. I'll roll up

to the final showdown with my chrome valentine DARPA,
who's worried that Space Force will put her on

the blacklist for being old-school.
Everyone else is worried

the NSC will put heads on pikes, strictly
for a counterfeit pillbox hat collection.

You gotta hand it to me
as a free agent sleeping

with MI6's in-demand sibling, I've set off
an international manhunt. Interpol, you won't call it off, would you?

(poem against the apparatus)

I spy
with my potato eye
with my eyewitness news cherub cannonball found in Hong Kong eye
with my mother hen eye to peck all the other eyes bloody. the wheel
        of order, or revolution, and all that
with my flash frozen banana eye
with my eight thousand fractal eyes eye
with my uranium eye
        which is also nuclear, and emits alpha particles,
        and which my third eye keeps an eye on
with my eye with steampunk gears of war in it
with my cherry glass heart eye
with my where you rolling off to
        with that retinal scanner,
        steve? eye
with my eye that wants blepharoplasty if penguins have triple eyelids so can
eye
with my backup evil eye
with my eye of the beholder, Thou whom the Speaker sees
        what Thou is whispering over there,
        reading me for filth eye

with my infinite Finnish leek stalk-swinging eye

with my organ-rearranging eye

with my arsonist's manual eye (rotate

      manually lest you get fired eye)

with my mermaid pissing a pool algae green eye

with my blackhearted rotten egg from the mother hen of all mothers eye

with my invisible eye

      that's the reason the illuminated bible's always screaming

      fear not.

(Dramatic Monologue as Shi Pei Pu)

After being married to your sunburned childhood
sweetheart, the French Embassy, for xx years, you'd think a little
peace from backseat driving is finally deserved. But no.

The plinky harp of counterintelligence goes on in perpetuity.
I brought down the heavens on my husband for making me
run yellow lights. On my skin? During Beijing Opera season?

Every primordial rib and chaotic theory has been acid-etched
on the honeycomb disco of my Double Stuf chrysalis. Every enemy camp
stitched on my gloving cheongsam. Every code I passed,

and the male guards always let me pass. I ate good
jade in the clothes of a lowly peasant cabbage and flossed
with archangel's gut and brass. I used no drugs or prophylactics

to fascinate both men and women. For two decades we were strung out
like paper lanterns, or vintage rice parasols. Love is sending us
up with no other forms of protection. I have that oyster grit but you,

the suicidal thoughts of a meat cleaver. I hit that
concubine's high note first and dragged myself out
long as the molting west was bottle green. Stuntmen are wholly good

for two things: missing your redacted's birthday and
bombshelling Hong Kong orange. Nothing tells me what I was
and what they were didn't matter.

(poem lined with double agents)

this is how to be a spook, if you know what's good for your aging stars,
foolproof and Asian,

007 in a land where honeybees are near-extinct, and of legal age. look
this one up—a Chinese harpoon woos

the last foxy paper magnate. this poem oozes without moonmen
or goddess. when everyone thinks spies, they think soba or hooker noodles

in Brooklyn, or cloistering by way of the woods with condoms and tarp.
know this—mushrooms and the poor are censored the same out here, and unlike

cowboys, more snaggletoothed austin than world powers, no one's
        sharpshooting villains
in the face. a farm in virginia called, and they're going footloose without
        chicken coops.

the raw flanks names a senator crooked for their fuzzy handcuff emoji o-o
        (cougar, you get it). there's something here
to be said about bamboo growing wilder than misunderstanding. james b needs
        to stop karate chopping people in the neck. your streetfighter record is 0-0

and don't throw away the receipt. you're a doomsdayer raccoon—gain weight
        and gain confidences,
and you won't need a blood pact to goose Florida's president.

(another one to yahoo). the only use of a boxing glove is to camouflage giant
        walnuts, and facebook tells you to this is how to hunt squirrels.
jason b has the Cool Whip and loom on lock, but gunfights are no gunfight
        and really you're on the run. so what do you do? if it's a private eye,

scissor the plastic you married, spoof your cheekbones, dye your hair with
        violent goo, buy a train ticket north, ride a greyhound south and hitchhike
west. and find a hoodie because you're more-faced than the Ghent Altarpiece.
        if it's the UN's booster seat, the nation-state and Us Weekly scoop you in
        48 hours. how to lose a guy

in seven rookie minutes? find a café, bribe the busboy, and you've bought yourself
        a backdoor hour or a micro-orgasm. hey, as long as you find the spot
        with targeted apps these days, it's anyone's school-game.

PIDGIN

Re: M. Moore

This is the mess.
This is the age we wrought.

This is the mess-age
and it's taken

ages to get it
to you through all these

waves, on
the fields, overseas

(and don't shoot the messenger)
but I will leave it here for you to read

next time.

Acknowledgements

All my gratitude to my teachers Doug Powell, Shane McCrae, Hanif Abdurraqib, Cy Jillian Weise, Jim Galvin, Robyn Schiff, Jorie Graham, Josh Bell, Ju Yon Kim, Golda Vainberg-Tatz, Lois Refkin, Pat Martinez, and the heart of the Iowa Writers Workshop, Sam Chang and Connie Brothers.

All my love to Priyanka Sen and Jason Gomez, Esteban Madrigal, Darara Bediso Borodge, my dear reader Jack Jung, and Samuel Lipoff. Thank you to Danez Smith, Kay Ullanday-Barrett and Devon Walker-Figueroa. I am thankful for the Poetry Incubator, and the faculty and students at the Tin House Workshop.

All my thanks to Timothy Liu and the editors at Saturnalia Press for believing in this manuscript, and the editors of the journals in which these poems previously appeared.

Pineapple (Narrative Magazine)

Who'd rob god? (Cortland Review)

Fu er dai (Poetry Northwest)

Bandaids didn't make a color for me, or Thinking inside the box, or Crayon within the lines (BOAAT)

Pomelo (Colorado Review)

Not Your Bernini's Daphne (Missouri Review)

Pyramid Scheme (South Carolina Review)

Everything about you is offensive except your cat (Colorado Review)

bye bye (Florida Review)

One child policy is the party pickup line (Cortland Review)

Antimatter (Colorado Review)

search engine (The Journal)

Modes of Production (Poetry Northwest)

How can you tell if it's ripe yet? (Cosmonauts Avenue)

Go big or go home (LA Review of Books)

to bear false whiteness (Frontier)

Buddha Discovers Reincarnation and Reaches Nirvana Under the Fig Tree's

Heart-Shaped Leaves (Indiana Review)

Multiple worlds interpretation (South Carolina Review)

Oregon 1945 (Narrative Magazine)

Outside party lines (Bennington Review)

While I'm not a heroic couplet (Verse Daily)

Quid Pro Nil (Missouri Review)

To scare men (South Carolina Review)

Nanjing 1937-38 (Tinderbox)

Advocacy (Poetry Northwest)

Halloween Redux (Tupelo Quarterly)

Matryoshka (Copper Nickel)

Deportation (Bennington Review)

The sign for power (Columbia Journal)

disinformation tactics (Iowa Review)

anything else would be off-brand (The Common)

poem against the apparatus (Iowa Review)

poem lined with double agents (KGB Literary Journal)

we begin bombing in 5 minutes (KGB Literary Journal)

Dramatic Monologue as Shi Pei Pu (Iowa Review)

Pidgin (The Common)

Spooks is printed in Adobe Caslon Pro.
www.saturnaliabooks.org